## Meet Holly Fields

Ask Holly Fields about her favorite things to crochet and she'll tell you they're usually "cute and tiny."

"I love to make baby clothes and doll items," Holly explains. "To create something detailed yet small is so gratifying. I find inspiration in color. I love to play with crayons or paint, just experimenting to see which colors look good together. I enjoy lovely textures, too. That's why I prefer to crochet with fine yarn or thread, so the texture of the stitches will really be visible."

Several of Holly's designs have appeared in magazines, and she has a book of designs for fashion dolls. She is a wife and proud mom who says, "I learned to crochet when I was a child, but it wasn't until my son came along many years later that I got really excited about crocheting."

Holly also likes to pamper Rudy, her sweet-natured German Shepherd. When she has time, she reads literature and the history of royalty. "I can never get enough of traveling," she says, "and England is my favorite country to visit."

# Playtime Jackets

*How adorable! Four toddler jackets and one little vest, all with cute motifs added! Each delightful pattern is sized for 12-, 18-, and 24-months. Make a Monkey sweater for a wee one whose antics make you smile. Stitch a classic Bead Toy appliqué to a shoulder-button cardigan. Fairy Tale Forest is an imaginative design with ruffles and mushroom appliqués, while Ice Cream is an extra-sweet confection in Neapolitan colors. And which would you crochet first for Breakfast on the Farm - the chicken or the eggs? You'll enjoy fashioning these fun garments almost as much as Baby will enjoy wearing them!*

## What's Inside




**LEISURE ARTS, INC.**
**Little Rock, Arkansas**

# Bead Toy

INTERMEDIATE

| Sizes | Finished Chest Measurement (Buttoned) | |
|---|---|---|
| 12 months | 20½" | (52 cm) |
| 18 months | 21¾" | (55 cm) |
| 24 months | 23" | (58.5 cm) |

***Size Note:*** Instructions are written for size 12 months, with sizes 18 and 24 months in braces { }. Instructions will be easier to read if you circle all the numbers pertaining to your size. If only one number is given, it applies to all sizes.

## Materials

MEDIUM 4

Medium Weight Yarn
- [6 ounces, 315 yards (170 grams, 287 meters) per skein]:
  - MC (White) - 1{1-2} skein(s)
- [3 ounces, 157 yards (85 grams, 144 meters) per skein]:
  - Color A (Pink) - 1 skein
  - Color B (Blue) - small amount

***Note:*** Reverse Colors A and B for Boy's Sweater.

Bedspread Weight Cotton Thread (size 10) **or** embroidery floss: small amount black for bead face

Crochet hook, size G (4 mm) **or** size needed for gauge

Tapestry needle

Sewing needle and thread

¾" (19 mm) Buttons - 2

1/8" (3 mm) wide Satin Ribbon - 6" (15 cm)

**Gauge:** In pattern, 9 dc = 2" (5 cm)
8 rows = 3" (7.5 cm)

**Gauge Swatch:** 2½" x 3" (6.5 cm x 7.5 cm)
Ch 14.
Work same as Body for 8 rows.
Finish off.

## Stitch Guide

### Decrease

Pull up a loop in each of next 2 sc, YO and draw through all 3 loops on hook **(counts as one sc)**.

## Body

Body is worked in one piece to underarm.

With MC, ch 116{125-134}.

**Row 1:** Sc in second ch from hook, (ch 2, skip next 2 chs, sc in next ch) across: 39{42-45} sc and 38{41-44} ch-2 sps.

**Row 2** (Right side)**:** Ch 3 **(counts as first dc, now and throughout)**, turn; dc in first sc, skip next ch-2 sp, (3 dc in next sc, skip next ch-2 sp) across to last sc, 2 dc in last sc: 115{124-133} dc.

Loop a short piece of yarn around any stitch to mark Row 2 as **right** side.

**Row 3:** Ch 1, turn; sc in first dc, (ch 2, skip next 2 dc, sc in next dc) across: 39{42-45} sc and 38{41-44} ch-2 sps.

**Rows 4 thru 13{15-15}:** Repeat Rows 2 and 3, 5{6-6} times; do **not** finish off.

The buttons will be sewn to the Left Front on the Girl's jacket, with the Right Front almost as wide as the Back and 2 buttonholes at the top neck edge. The Fronts for the Boy's jacket are worked the opposite, and the Back is worked the same.

### Girl's Right Front

**Row 1:** Ch 3, turn; dc in first sc, skip next ch-2 sp, (3 dc in next sc, skip next ch-2 sp) 13{14-15} times, 2 dc in next sc, leave remaining sts unworked: 43{46-49} dc.

**Row 2:** Ch 1, turn; sc in first dc, (ch 2, skip next 2 dc, sc in next dc) across: 15{16-17} sc and 14{15-16} ch-2 sps.

**Row 3:** Ch 3, turn; dc in first sc, skip next ch-2 sp, (3 dc in next sc, skip next ch-2 sp) across to last sc, 2 dc in last sc: 43{46-49} dc.

**Size 12 months Only - Row 4:** Repeat Row 2.

**Sizes 18 and 24 months Only - Rows 4 thru {6-8}:** Repeat Rows 2 and 3, {1-2} times; then repeat Row 2 once **more**.

### All Sizes

**Buttonhole Row:** Ch 3, turn; skip next ch-2 sp to create buttonhole, (3 dc in next sc, skip next ch-2 sp) across to last sc, 2 dc in last sc: 42{45-48} dc.

**Next Row:** Ch 1, turn; sc in first dc, (ch 2, skip next 2 dc, sc in next dc) across to last 2 dc, ch 2, skip next dc, sc in last dc: 15{16-17} sc and 14{15-16} ch-2 sps.

**Next Row:** Repeat Buttonhole Row; do **not** finish off.

### Neck Shaping

**Row 1:** Ch 1, turn; sc in first dc, (ch 2, skip next 2 dc, sc in next dc) 3{4-5} times, leave remaining sts unworked: 4{5-6} sc and 3{4-5} ch-2 sps.

**Row 2:** Ch 3, turn; dc in first sc, skip next ch-2 sp, (3 dc in next sc, skip next ch-2 sp) across to last sc, 2 dc in last sc: 10{13-16} dc.

**Row 3:** Ch 1, turn; sc in first dc, (ch 2, skip next 2 dc, sc in next dc) across: 4{5-6} sc and 3{4-5} ch-2 sps.

**Row 4:** Repeat Row 2; finish off leaving a long length for sewing.

### Boy's Right Front

**Row 1:** Ch 3, turn; dc in first sc, skip next ch-2 sp, (3 dc in next sc, skip next ch-2 sp) 6{7-8} times, 2 dc in next sc, leave remaining sts unworked: 22{25-28} dc.

**Row 2:** Ch 1, turn; sc in first dc, (ch 2, skip next 2 dc, sc in next dc) across: 8{9-10} sc and 7{8-9} ch-2 sps.

**Row 3:** Ch 3, turn; dc in first sc, skip next ch-2 sp, (3 dc in next sc, skip next ch-2 sp) across to last sc, 2 dc in last sc: 22{25-28} dc.

**Rows 4 thru 7{9-11}:** Repeat Rows 2 and 3, 2{3-4} times.

### Neck Shaping

**Row 1:** Ch 1, turn; sc in first dc, (ch 2, skip next 2 dc, sc in next dc) 3{4-5} times, leave remaining sts unworked: 4{5-6} sc and 3{4-5} ch-2 sps.

**Row 2:** Ch 3, turn; dc in first sc, skip next ch-2 sp, (3 dc in next sc, skip next ch-2 sp) across, 2 dc in last sc: 10{13-16} dc.

**Row 3:** Ch 1, turn; sc in first dc, (ch 2, skip next 2 dc, sc in next dc) across: 4{5-6} sc and 3{4-5} ch-2 sps.

**Row 4:** Repeat Row 2; finish off leaving a long length for sewing.

### BACK (GIRL'S AND BOY'S)

**Row 1:** With **right** side facing, skip first ch-2 sp after Right Front and join MC with dc in next sc ***(see Joining With Dc, page 30)***, dc in same st, skip next ch-2 sp, (3 dc in next sc, skip next ch-2 sp) 14{15-16} times, 2 dc in next sc, leave remaining sts unworked: 46{49-52} dc.

**Row 2:** Ch 1, turn; sc in first dc, (ch 2, skip next 2 dc, sc in next dc) across: 16{17-18} sc and 15{16-17} ch-2 sps.

**Row 3:** Ch 3, turn; dc in first sc, skip next ch-2 sp, (3 dc in next sc, skip next ch-2 sp) across to last sc, 2 dc in last sc: 46{49-52} dc.

**Rows 4 thru 11{13-15}:** Repeat Rows 2 and 3, 4{5-6} times.

Finish off.

### GIRL'S LEFT FRONT

**Row 1:** With **right** side facing, skip first ch-2 sp after Back and join MC with dc in next sc, dc in same st, skip next ch-2 sp, (3 dc in next sc, skip next ch-2 sp) across to last sc, 2 dc in last sc: 22{25-28} dc.

**Row 2:** Ch 1, turn; sc in first dc, (ch 2, skip next 2 dc, sc in next dc) across: 8{9-10} sc and 7{8-9} ch-2 sps.

**Row 3:** Ch 3, turn; dc in first sc, skip next ch-2 sp, (3 dc in next sc, skip next ch-2 sp) across to last sc, 2 dc in last sc: 22{25-28} dc.

**Rows 4 thru 7{9-11}:** Repeat Rows 2 and 3, 2{3-4} times.

### NECK SHAPING

**Row 1:** Turn; slip st in first 12 dc, ch 1, sc in next dc, (ch 2, skip next 2 dc, sc in next dc) across: 4{5-6} sc and 3{4-5} ch-2 sps.

**Row 2:** Ch 3, turn; dc in first sc, skip next ch-2 sp, (3 dc in next sc, skip next ch-2 sp) across to last sc, 2 dc in last sc: 10{13-16} dc.

**Row 3:** Ch 1, turn; sc in first dc, (ch 2, skip next 2 dc, sc in next dc) across: 4{5-6} sc and 3{4-5} ch-2 sps.

**Row 4:** Repeat Row 2; finish off leaving a long length for sewing.

### BOY'S LEFT FRONT

**Row 1:** With **right** side facing, skip first ch-2 sp after Back and join MC with dc in next sc, dc in same st, skip next ch-2 sp, (3 dc in next sc, skip next ch-2 sp) across to last sc, 2 dc in last sc: 43{46-49} dc.

**Row 2:** Ch 1, turn; sc in first dc, (ch 2, skip next 2 dc, sc in next dc) across: 15{16-17} sc and 14{15-16} ch-2 sps.

**Row 3:** Ch 3, turn; dc in first sc, skip next ch-2 sp, (3 dc in next sc, skip next ch-2 sp) across to last sc, 2 dc in last sc: 43{46-49} dc.

**Size 12 Months Only - Row 4:** Repeat Row 2.

**Sizes 18 and 24 Months Only - Rows 4 thru {6-8}:** Repeat Rows 2 and 3, {1-2} times; then repeat Row 2 once **more**.

### ALL SIZES

**Buttonhole Row:** Ch 3, turn; dc in first sc, skip next ch-2 sp, (3 dc in next sc, skip next ch-2 sp) across to last sc, dc in last sc to create buttonhole: 42{45-48} dc.

**Next Row:** Ch 1, turn; sc in first dc, ch 2, skip next dc, sc in next dc, (ch 2, skip next 2 dc, sc in next dc) across: 15{16-17} sc and 14{15-16} ch-2 sps.

**Next Row:** Repeat Buttonhole Row; do **not** finish off.

### Neck Shaping

**Row 1:** Turn; slip st in first 32 dc, ch 1, sc in next dc, (ch 2, skip next 2 dc, sc in next dc) across: 4{5-6} sc and 3{4-5} ch-2 sps.

**Row 2:** Ch 3, turn; dc in first sc, skip next ch-2 sp, (3 dc in next sc, skip next ch-2 sp) across to last sc, 2 dc in last sc: 10{13-16} dc.

**Row 3:** Ch 1, turn; sc in first dc, (ch 2, skip next 2 dc, sc in next dc) across: 4{5-6} sc and 3{4-5} ch-2 sps.

**Row 4:** Repeat Row 2; finish off leaving a long length for sewing.

Whipstitch shoulder seams ***(Fig. 5, page 31)***.

### Edging

With **right** side facing and working in free loops of beginning ch ***(Fig. 2, page 30)***, join Color A with sc in first ch (***see Joining With Sc, page 30)***; 2 sc in same st, sc in next ch and in each ch across to last ch, 3 sc in last ch; sc evenly spaced around working 2 sc in each buttonhole and 3 sc in each top corner of neck edge; join with slip st to first sc; finish off.

### Sleeve (make 2)

Sleeve is worked across length.

With MC, ch 35{38-41}.

**Row 1:** Sc in second ch from hook, (ch 2, skip next 2 chs, sc in next ch) across: 12{13-14} sc and 11{12-13} ch-2 sps.

**Row 2** (Right side)**:** Ch 3, turn; dc in first sc, skip next ch-2 sp, (3 dc in next sc, skip next ch-2 sp) across to last sc, 2 dc in last sc: 34{37-40} dc.

**Row 3:** Ch 1, turn; sc in first dc, (ch 2, skip next 2 dc, sc in next dc) across: 12{13-14} sc and 11{12-13} ch-2 sps.

**Rows 4 thru 21{25-29}:** Repeat Rows 2 and 3, 9{11-13} times.

Finish off leaving a long length for sewing.

With **right** sides together, fold Sleeve in half and whipstitch seam, matching last row to beginning ch; whipstitch Sleeve to armhole, placing seam at bottom of armhole and easing to fit.

## Edging

With **right** side facing and working in end of rows on Sleeve, join Color A with sc in first row; (2 sc in next row, sc in next row) around; join with slip st to first sc; finish off: 31{37-43} sc.

## Finishing

Sew buttons to Front opposite buttonholes, making sure to sew them on firmly so baby cannot pull them off.

## Bead Appliqué

### Body

**Rnd 1:** With Color A, ch 2, 6 sc in second ch from hook; join with slip st to first sc.

**Rnd 2:** Ch 1, 2 sc in each sc around; join with slip st to first sc: 12 sc.

**Rnd 3:** Ch 1, 2 sc in first sc, sc in next sc, (2 sc in next sc, sc in next sc) around; join with slip st to first sc: 18 sc.

**Rnd 4:** Ch 1, 2 sc in first sc, sc in next 2 sc, (2 sc in next sc, sc in next 2 sc) around, join with slip st to first sc: 24 sc.

**Rnd 5:** Ch 1, 2 sc in first sc, sc in next 3 sc, (2 sc in next sc, sc in next 3 sc) around; join with slip st to first sc; finish off leaving a long length for sewing: 30 sc.

### Head

**Rnds 1-3:** Work same as Body.

Finish off leaving a long length for sewing: 18 sc.

### Leg (make 2)

With Color B, ch 2, 6 sc in second ch from hook; join with slip st to first sc, ★ ch 3, 6 sc in second ch from hook; join with slip st to first sc, slip st in each of next 2 sc; repeat from ★ once **more**; finish off leaving a long length for sewing.

### Arm (make 2)

With Color B, ch 2, 6 sc in second ch from hook; join with slip st to first sc, ch 3, 6 sc in second ch from hook; join with slip st to first sc; finish off leaving a long length for sewing.

### Hat

With Color B, ch 7.

**Row 1:** Sc in second ch from hook and in each ch across: 6 sc.

**Row 2:** Ch 1, turn; decrease, sc in next 2 sc, decrease: 4 sc.

**Row 3:** Ch 1, turn; decrease twice; finish off leaving a long length for sewing: 2 sc.

**Pompom:** With Color A, ch 2, 6 sc in second ch from hook; join with slip st to first sc; finish off leaving a long length for sewing.

**Face:** Using black crochet thread or embroidery floss and tapestry needle, embroider facial features using Backstitch ***(Fig. 7, page 31)*** for mouth and French Knots ***(Fig. 6, page 31)*** for eyes and nose on lower half of Head only (Hat will cover upper half of Head).

Using photo as a guide for placement, pin all pieces to front of cardigan, then sew in place.

Tie ribbon in a bow; tack bow under chin; trim ends if necessary.

# Monkeying Around

INTERMEDIATE

| Sizes | Finished Chest Measurement (buttoned) | |
|---|---|---|
| 12 months | 21" | (53.5 cm) |
| 18 months | 22¼" | (56.5 cm) |
| 24 months | 23" | (58.5 cm) |

***Size Note:*** Instructions are written for size 12 months, with sizes 18 and 24 months in braces { }. Instructions will be easier to read if you circle all the numbers pertaining to your size. If only one number is given, it applies to all sizes.

## Materials

Cotton Thread (size 3):
[150 yards (137 meters) per ball]:
MC (Blue) - 5{6-7} balls

Bedspread Weight Cotton Thread (size 10):
[320 yards (292 meters) per ball]:
Tan - small amount
Cream - small amount
Red - small amount

Crochet hooks, sizes B (2.25 mm) **and** E (3.5 mm) **or** sizes needed for gauge

Tapestry needle

Sewing needle and thread

5/8" (16 mm) Shank buttons - 2

4 mm Black beads - 2

¼" (7 mm) wide Satin Ribbon - 8" (20.5 cm)

**Gauge:** In pattern: With size 3 cotton thread and larger size hook, 12 sc and 17 rows = 2" (5 cm); With size 10 cotton thread and smaller size hook, 16 sc and 20 rows or rnds = 2" (5 cm)

**Gauge Swatch:** 2" (5 cm) square
Ch 13.
Work same as Back for 17 rows.
Finish off.

## Stitch Guide

### Spike Sc

Working **around** previous row ***(Fig. 3, page 31)***, insert hook in st in row **below** next sc, YO and pull up a loop, YO and draw through both loops on hook.

### Decrease

Pull up a loop in each of next 2 sc, YO and draw through all 3 loops on hook **(counts as one sc)**.

## Back

With larger size hook and MC, ch 64{68-70}.

**Row 1:** Sc in second ch from hook and in each ch across: 63{67-69} sc.

**Row 2** (Right side)**:** Ch 1, turn; sc in each sc across.

Loop a short piece of yarn around any stitch to mark Row 2 as **right** side.

**Row 3:** Ch 1, turn; sc in first sc, (work Spike sc sc in next st) across.

R

**Row 4:** Ch 1, turn; work Spike sc, (sc in next st, work Spike sc) across.

**Rows 5 thru 58{62-66}:** Repeat Rows 3 and 4, 27{29-31} times.

Finish off.

## Right Front

With larger size hook and MC, ch 30{32-34}.

**Row 1:** Sc in second ch from hook and in each ch across: 29{31-33} sc.

Work same as Back for a total of 48{52-56} rows.

## Neck Shaping

**Row 1** (Decrease row)**:** Ch 1, turn; sc in first sc, (work Spike sc, sc in next sc) across to last 4 sc, decrease twice: 27{29-31} sts.

**Row 2** (Decrease row)**:** Ch 1, turn; decrease twice, work Spike sc, (sc in next st, work Spike sc) across: 25{27-29} sts.

**Rows 3-9:** Repeat Rows 1 and 2, 3 times; then repeat Row 1 once **more**: 11{13-15} sts.

**Row 10:** Ch 1, turn; sc in each st across; finish off leaving a long length for sewing.

## Left Front

Work same as Right Front, marking Row 1 as **right** side.

## Sleeve (make 2)

With larger size hook and MC, ch 56{58-64}.

**Row 1** (Right side)**:** Sc in second ch from hook and in each ch across: 55{57-63} sc.

Mark Row 1 as **right** side.

Work same as Back for a total of 56{60-64} rows.

Finish off leaving a long length for sewing.

## Finishing

Whipstitch shoulder seams ***(Fig. 5, page 31)***.

Whipstitch Sleeves to cardigan, matching center of last row on Sleeve to shoulder seam and beginning 4½{4¾-5¼}" (11.5{12-13.5} cm) down from seam.

Whipstitch Sleeve and side in one continuous seam.

## Cuff

**Rnd 1:** With **right** side facing, using larger size hook, and working in free loops of beginning ch ***(Fig. 2, page 30)***, join MC with sc in first ch; sc in next 54{56-62} chs; join with slip st to first sc: 55{57-63} sc.

**Rnd 2:** Ch 1, do **not** turn; sc in first 5{11-7} sc, decrease, (sc in next 4{9-7} sc, decrease) around; join with slip st to first sc: 46{52-56} sc.

**Rnd 3:** Ch 1, sc in first 2{5-5} sc, decrease, (sc in next 4{7-5} sc, decrease) around; join with slip st to first sc: 38{46-48} sc.

**Rnd 4:** Ch 1, sc in first 1{4-4} sc, decrease, (sc in next 3{6-4} sc, decrease) around; join with slip st to first sc: 30{40-40} sc.

**Rnd 5:** Ch 1, sc in each sc around; join with slip st to first sc; finish off.

Repeat for second Sleeve.

## Edging

**Row 1:** With **right** side facing and working in end of rows, join MC with sc in row before Neck Shaping on Left Front ***(see Joining With Sc, page 30)***; work 40{44-48} sc evenly spaced across to corner; working in free loops of beginning ch, 3 sc in first ch, sc in each ch across to last ch, 3 sc in last ch; work 40{44-48} sc evenly spaced across end of rows to Right Front Neck Shaping.

**Rows 2-4:** Ch 1, turn; decrease, (sc in each sc across to center sc of next corner 3-sc group, 3 sc in center sc) twice, sc in each sc across to last 2 sc, decrease.

**Girl's Only - Row 5** (Buttonhole row)**:** Ch 1, turn; decrease, (sc in each sc across to center sc of next corner 3-sc group, 3 sc in center sc) twice, sc in each sc across to last 11 sc, ch 3, skip next 3 sc, sc in next 3 sc, ch 3, skip next 3 sc, decrease.

**Boy's Only - Row 5** (Buttonhole row)**:** Ch 1, turn; decrease, ch 3, skip next 3 sc, sc in next 3 sc, ch 3, skip next 3 sc, (sc in each sc across to center sc of next corner 3-sc group, 3 sc in center sc) twice, sc in each sc across to last 2 sc, decrease.

**Both Girl's and Boy's - Row 6:** Ch 1, turn; sc in each sc across, working 3 sc in each ch-3 sp (buttonhole) and 3 sc in center sc of each corner 3-sc group; do **not** finish off.

## Collar

**Row 1:** With **wrong** side facing, sc evenly across end of rows on Left Front Edging and Neck Shaping; sc in each st across Back neck edge; sc evenly across end of rows on Right Front Neck Shaping and Edging; slip st in first sc on Row 6 of Edging.

**Row 2:** Ch 1, turn; sc in Front Loop Only of each sc across ***(Fig. 1, page 30)***.

**Rows 3 thru 10{12-14}:** Ch 1, turn; sc in **both** loops of each sc across.

Finish off.

Fold Collar down.

Sew buttons to Front opposite buttonholes, making sure to sew them on firmly so baby cannot pull them off.

## Monkey Appliqué

Use smaller size hook and size 10 cotton thread throughout appliqué.

### Head

With Tan, ch 10.

**Foundation Rnd** (Right side)**:** 3 sc in second ch from hook, sc in next ch, hdc in next ch, dc in next 3 chs, hdc in next ch, sc in next ch, 4 sc in last ch; working in free loops on opposite side of beginning ch, sc in next ch, hdc in next ch, dc in next 3 chs, hdc in next ch, sc in next 2 chs; join with slip st to first sc: 22 sts.

Mark Foundation Rnd as **right** side.

**Row 1:** Ch 1, turn; skip sc joined into, sc in next 10 sts, leave remaining sts unworked: 10 sc.

**Row 2:** Ch 1, turn; decrease, sc in next 6 sc, decrease: 8 sc.

**Rows 3 and 4:** Ch 1, turn; sc in each sc across.

**Row 5:** Ch 1, turn; 2 sc in first sc, sc in next 6 sc, 2 sc in last sc: 10 sc.

**Rows 6-8:** Ch 1, turn; sc in each sc across.

**Rows 9-11:** Ch 1, turn; decrease, sc in next sc and in each sc across to last 2 sc, decrease: 4 sc.

**Row 12:** Ch 1, turn; decrease twice: 2 sc.

**Edging:** Ch 1, do **not** turn; sc evenly around entire piece; join with slip st to first sc; finish off.

### Muzzle

With Cream, ch 10.

Work same as Foundation Rnd on Head; finish off leaving a long length for sewing.

### Ear (make 2)

With Tan, ch 4.

**Row 1:** 2 Sc in second ch from hook, 3 dc in next ch, 2 sc in last ch: 7 sts.

**Row 2:** Ch 1, turn; sc in each st across; finish off leaving a long length for sewing.

## MOUTH

With Red, ch 7, leaving a long length for sewing; finish off.

Using photo as a guide for placement, sew Mouth to Muzzle, forming a smile. Sew Muzzle to lower part of Head and sew Ears to sides of Head. Sew beads (for eyes) to Head just above Muzzle.

## HAT

With Red, ch 11.

**Row 1:** Sc in second ch from hook and in each ch across: 10 sc.

**Row 2:** Ch 1, turn; decrease, sc in next 6 sc, decrease: 8 sc.

**Rows 3 and 4:** Ch 1, turn; decrease, sc in each sc across to last 2 sc, decrease: 4 sc.

**Row 5:** Ch 1, turn; decrease twice: 2 sc.

**Edging** (Right side)**:** Ch 1, turn; sc evenly around entire piece; join with slip st to first sc; do **not** finish off.

**Hat Topper:** (Ch 3, 2 dc, ch 3, slip st) twice in same sc; finish off leaving a long length for sewing.

Sew Hat over top 5 rows of Head.

## BODY

With Tan, ch 8.

**Row 1:** Sc in second ch from hook and in each ch across: 7 sc.

**Row 2** (Right side)**:** Ch 1, turn; sc in each sc across.

Mark Row 2 as **right** side.

**Row 3** (Increase row)**:** Ch 1, turn; 2 sc in first sc, sc in each sc across to last sc, 2 sc in last sc: 9 sc.

**Rows 4-7:** Repeat Rows 2 and 3, twice: 13 sc.

**Rows 8-17:** Ch 1, turn; sc in each sc across; do **not** finish off.

## RIGHT LEG

**Row 1:** Ch 1, turn; sc in first 5 sc, leave remaining 8 sc unworked: 5 sc.

**Rows 2-12:** Ch 1, turn; sc in each sc across. Finish off.

## LEFT LEG

**Row 1:** With **right** side of Body facing, skip 3 sc from First Leg and join Tan with sc in next sc; sc in last 4 sc: 5 sc.

**Rows 2-12:** Ch 1, turn; sc in each sc across. Finish off.

## Right Arm

**Row 1:** With **right** side of Body facing and working in end of rows, join Tan with sc in Row 3; sc in next 3 rows working toward legs: 4 sc.

**Rows 2-10:** Ch 1, turn; sc in each sc across. Finish off.

## Tail

**Row 1:** With **right** side of Body facing, skip 7 rows from Right Arm and join Tan with sc in next row; sc in next row: 2 sc.

**Rows 2-6:** Ch 1, turn; sc in each sc across.

**Row 7:** Ch 1, turn; 2 sc in first sc, leave last sc unworked: 2 sc.

**Rows 8-15:** Ch 1, turn; sc in each sc across. Finish off.

## Left Arm

**Row 1:** With **right** side of Body facing and working in end of rows, join Tan with sc in Row 6; sc in next 3 rows working toward neck: 4 sc.

**Rows 2-10:** Ch 1, turn; sc in each sc across. Do **not** finish off.

**Edging:** With **right** side facing, ch 1, sc evenly around entire piece, join with slip st to first sc; finish off leaving a long length for sewing.

## Hand (Make 2)

**Row 1:** With **right** side facing, join Cream with sc at end of Arm; sc in next 4 sc: 5 sc.

**Row 2:** Ch 1, turn; sc in each sc across.

**Row 3:** Ch 1, turn; decrease, sc in next sc, decrease: 3 sc.

**Row 4:** Ch 1, turn; sc in each sc across.

**Row 5:** Ch 1, turn; pull up a loop in each sc, YO and draw through all 4 loops on hook; finish off.

## Foot

**Row 1:** With **right** side facing, join Cream with sc at end of Leg; sc in next 6 sc: 7 sc.

**Row 2:** Ch 1, turn; sc in each sc across.

**Row 3:** Ch 1, turn; decrease, sc in next 3 sc, decrease: 5 sc.

**Row 4:** Ch 1, turn; sc in each sc across.

**Row 5:** Ch 1, turn; decrease, sc in next sc, decrease: 3 sc.

**Row 6:** Ch 1, turn; sc in each sc across.

**Row 7:** Ch 1, turn; pull up a loop in each sc, YO and draw through all 4 loops on hook; finish off.

Repeat for second Foot.

## Tip of Tail

**Row 1:** With **right** side facing, join Cream with sc at end of Tail; sc in next 2 sc: 3 sc.

**Rows 2-4:** Ch 1, turn; sc in each sc across.

**Row 5:** Ch 1, turn; pull up a loop in each of first 3 sc, YO and draw through all 4 loops on hook; finish off.

Using photo as a guide for placement, pin Monkey's Head and Body to Left Front of cardigan. Sew in place.

Tie the ribbon in a bow and sew to Monkey's neck.

# Breakfast on the Farm

EXPERIENCED

| Sizes | Finished Chest Measurement (buttoned) | |
|---|---|---|
| 12 months | 22½" | (57 cm) |
| 18 months | 24" | (61 cm) |
| 24 months | 25¼" | (64 cm) |

***Size Note:*** Instructions are written for size 12 months, with sizes 18 and 24 months in braces { }. Instructions will be easier to read if you circle all the numbers pertaining to your size. If only one number is given, it applies to all sizes.

## Materials

FINE 2

Fine Weight Yarn
[4 ounces, 335 yards
(113 grams, 306 meters) per skein]:
MC (Red) - 1{1-2} skein(s)
Color A (White) - 1 skein
Color B (Yellow) - small amount
Color C (Black) - small amount
Crochet hook, size F (3.75 mm) **or** size needed for gauge
Tapestry needle
Sewing needle and thread
5/8" (16 mm) Buttons - 6

**Gauge:** 15 sc and 13 rows = 2" (5 cm)

**Gauge Swatch:** 2" (5 cm) square
Ch 16.
**Row 1:** Sc in second ch from hook and in each ch across.
**Rows 2-13:** Ch 1, turn; sc in each sc across. Finish off.

## Stitch Guide

### Decrease

Pull up a loop in each of next 2 sc, YO and draw through all 3 loops on hook **(counts as one sc)**.

## Body

With MC, ch 25.
**Row 1:** Sc in second ch from hook and in each ch across: 24 sc.
**Rows 2-150{155-170}:** Ch 1, turn; sc in Back Loop Only of each sc across ***(Fig. 1, page 30)***.
**Edging:** Ch 1, do **not** turn; sc in end of each row across working in free loops of beginning ch ***(Fig. 2, page 30)***, 2 sc in first ch, sc in each ch across to last ch, 2 sc in last ch; sc in end of each row across to last row, 1{2-1} sc in last row; working in Back Loops Only across Row 150{155-170}, 2 sc in first sc, sc in next sc and in each sc across to last sc, 2 sc in last sc; join with slip st to first sc; do **not** finish off.

## Left Front

Each color block is made up of 5 sc, which is worked for 5 rows.

**To change colors**, work last sc before color change to last step (2 loops on hook), drop yarn to **wrong** side; with new color, YO and draw through both loops on hook ***(Fig. 4, page 31)***. Work over yarn not being used.

**Row 1** (Wrong side)**:** Ch 1, do **not** turn; sc in first 5 sc changing to Color A, (sc in next 5 sc changing to MC, sc in next 5 sc changing to Color A) twice, sc in next 0{0-5} sc changing to MC ***(see Zeros, page 30)***, sc in next 5 sc, leave remaining sts unworked: 30{30-35} sc.

**Rows 2-5:** Ch 1, turn; sc in first 5 sc changing to next color, (sc in next 5 sc changing to next color) across to last 5 sc, sc in last 5 sc.

**Row 6:** With next color, ch 1, turn; sc in first 5 sc changing to next color, (sc in next 5 sc changing to next color) across. Colors are now reversed.

**Rows 7-10:** Ch 1, turn; sc in first 5 sc changing to next color, (sc in next 5 sc changing to next color) across to last 5 sc, sc in last 5 sc.

**Rows 11 thru 15{25-25}:** Repeat Rows 6-10, 1{3-3} times.

## Neck Shaping

**Row 1:** With next color, ch 1, turn; sc in first 5 sc changing to next color, (sc in next 5 sc changing to next color) across to last 10 sc, sc in next 5 sc, leave remaining 5 sc unworked: 25{25-30} sc.

**Rows 2-5:** Ch 1, turn; sc in first 5 sc changing to next color, (sc in next 5 sc changing to next color) across to last 5 sc, sc in last 5 sc.

**Row 6:** Turn; slip st in first 5 sc, ch 1, (sc in next 5 sc changing to next color) across to last 5 sc, sc in last 5 sc: 20{20-25} sc.

**Rows 7-10:** Ch 1, turn; sc in first 5 sc changing to next color, (sc in next 5 sc changing to next color) across to last 5 sc, sc in last 5 sc.

Finish off leaving a long length for sewing.

## Back

**Row 1:** With **wrong** side facing, skip next 5 sc from Left Front and join MC{MC-Color A} with sc in next sc ***(see Joining With Sc, page 30)***; sc in next 4 sc, (sc in next 5 sc changing to next color) 14{15-16} times, sc in next 5 sc, leave remaining sc unworked: 80{85-90} sc.

**Rows 2-5:** Ch 1, turn; sc in first 5 sc changing to next color, (sc in next 5 sc changing to next color) across to last 5 sc, sc in last 5 sc.

**Row 6:** With next color, ch 1, turn; sc in first 5 sc changing to next color, (sc in next 5 sc changing to next color) across.

**Rows 7-10:** Ch 1, turn; sc in first 5 sc changing to next color, (sc in next 5 sc changing to next color) across to last 5 sc, sc in last 5 sc.

**Rows 11 thru 25{35-35}:** Repeat Rows 6-10, 3{5-5} times.

Finish off leaving a long length for sewing.

### Right Front

**Row 1:** With **wrong** side facing, skip next 5 sc from Back; join MC{Color A-Color A} with sc in next sc, sc in next 4 sc, (sc in next 5 sc changing to next color) across to last 5 sc, sc in last 5 sc.

Work same as Left Front to Neck Shaping.

### Neck Shaping

**Row 1:** Turn; slip st in first 5 sc, ch 1, (sc in next 5 sc changing to next color) across to last 5 sc, sc in last 5 sc: 25{25-30} sc.

**Rows 2-5:** Ch 1, turn; sc in first 5 sc changing to next color, (sc in next 5 sc changing to next color) across to last 5 sc, sc in last 5 sc.

**Row 6:** With next color, ch 1, turn; sc in first 5 sc changing to next color, (sc in next 5 sc changing to next color) across to last 5 sts, leave remaining
5 sts unworked: 20{20-25} sc.

**Rows 7-10:** Ch 1, turn; sc in first 5 sc changing to next color, (sc in next 5 sc changing to next color) across to last 5 sc, sc in last 5 sc.

Finish off leaving a long length for sewing.

Whipstitch shoulder seams *(**Fig. 5, page 31**)*.

### Finishing

### Armhole Edging

With **right** side facing, join MC with sc in center sc at bottom of armhole; sc in next 2 sc, sc in end of each row around, sc in last 2 sc; join with slip st to first sc.

Repeat for second side.

### Neck Edging

With **right** side facing and working in end of rows, join MC with sc in first row of Right Front (checkered section), sc in each row across to Neck Shaping, 3 sc in corner, continue to sc in each sc and in each row around checkered section, working 3 sc in each outer corner; finish off.

### Button Placket

Work the Button Placket on the Left Front for a girl's vest and the Right Front for a boy's vest.

**Row 1:** With **right** side facing and working in Back Loops Only, join MC with sc in first sc on front opening; sc in each sc across Body and Front Neck Edging to Neck Shaping: 42{52-52} sc.

**Rows 2 thru 10{15-10}:** Ch 1, turn; sc in Back Loops Only of each sc across.

Finish off.

### Buttonhole Placket

**Row 1:** With **right** side facing and working in Back Loops Only, join MC with sc in first sc on the front opening of remaining side; sc in each sc across: 42{52-52} sc.

**Rows 2 thru 5:** Ch 1, turn; working in Back Loops Only, sc in each sc across.

**Row 6** (Buttonhole row)**:** Ch 1, turn; working in Back Loops Only, sc in first 3 sc, ch 3, skip next 3 sc, sc in next 14{19-19} sc, ch 3, skip next 3 sc, sc in next 13{18-18} sc, ch 3, skip next 3 sc, sc in last 3 sc.

**Row 7:** Ch 1, turn; working in Back Loops Only, sc in each sc across working 3 sc in each ch-3 sp: 42{47-52} sc.

**Rows 8 thru 9{14-9}:** Repeat Row 2.

**Rows 10{15-10} and 11{16-11}:** Repeat Rows 6 and 7.

**Rows 12{17-12} and 13{18-13}:** Repeat Row 2.

Finish off.

Sew buttons to Button Placket opposite buttonholes, making sure to sew them on firmly so baby cannot pull them off.

### Hen Appliqué

#### Body

With Color A, ch 11.

**Row 1:** Sc in second ch from hook and in each ch across: 10 sc.

**Row 2** (Right side, Increase row)**:** Ch 1, turn; 2 sc in first sc, sc in each sc across to last sc, 2 sc in last sc: 12 sc.

**Row 3:** Ch 1, turn; sc in each sc across.

**Row 4:** Repeat Row 2: 14 sc.

**Rows 5 and 6:** Ch 1, turn; sc in each sc across.

**Row 7** (Decrease row)**:** Ch 1, turn; decrease, sc in each sc across to last 2 sc, decrease: 12 sc.

**Rows 8 and 9:** Ch 1, turn; sc in each sc across.

**Row 10:** Repeat Row 7: 10 sc.

**Rows 11 and 12:** Ch 1, turn; sc in each sc across.

**Edging:** Ch 1, do **not** turn; sc in end of each row to beginning ch; ch 1, working in free loops of beginning ch, sc in each ch across; ch 1, sc in end of each row across to Row 12, ch 1, sc in each sc across Row 12; join with slip st to first sc; do **not** finish off.

**Tail Feathers:** Ch 7, sc in second ch from hook, hdc in next ch, dc in next 2 chs, tr in next 2 chs, skip next 4 sc on side of Hen's Body; join to Body with slip st in next sc; finish off leaving a long length for sewing.

## NECK

**Row 1:** With **right** side facing, join Color A with sc in sixth sc down right side of Hen's Body; sc in each sc up to top Row of Body: 6 sc.

**Row 2:** Ch 3, turn; skip first sc, dc in next 2 sc, hdc in next sc, sc in next sc, slip st in last sc; finish off.

## HEAD

**Rnd 1:** With Color A, ch 2, 6 sc in second ch from hook; join with slip st to first sc: 6 sc.

**Rnd 2:** Ch 1, do **not** turn; 2 sc in each sc around; join with slip st to first sc: 12 sc.

**Rnd 3:** Repeat Rnd 2; finish off leaving a long length for sewing: 24 sc.

Sew Head in place on Neck, using photo for placement.

## COMB

With **right** side facing, join Color B with slip st in fifth sc from neck on top of Head; (ch 8, sc in next sc) 4 times; finish off leaving a long length for sewing.

## BEAK

**Row 1:** With right side facing, join Color B with sc in seventh sc from Comb and in next 3 sc: 4 sc.

**Row 2:** Turn; decrease twice: 2 sc.

**Row 3:** Turn, decrease; finish off leaving a long length for sewing.

**Eye:** With Color C and tapestry needle, embroider a French Knot *(**Fig. 6, page 31**)* on Head using photo as a guide for placement.

Sew Hen appliqué to Right Front of vest.

When sewing on the Comb, attach only the lower Comb allowing the ch-8 loops to remain free.

## EGG APPLIQUÉ (MAKE 3)

With Color A, ch 7.

**Row 1** (Right side)**:** Sc in second ch from hook and in each ch across: 6 sc.

**Rows 2 and 3:** Ch 1, turn; 2 sc in first sc, sc in next sc and in each sc across to last sc, 2 sc in last sc: 10 sc.

**Row 4:** Ch 1, turn; sc in each sc across.

**Rows 5 and 6:** Ch 1, turn; decrease, sc in each sc across to last 2 sc, decrease: 6 sc.

**Edging:** Ch 1, sc evenly around; join with slip st to first sc; finish off leaving a long length for sewing.

Using photo as a guide for placement, pin Chicken to Right Front and Eggs to Left Front; then sew in place.

# Fairy Tale Forest

INTERMEDIATE

| Sizes | Finished Chest Measurement (excluding ruffle) | |
|---|---|---|
| 12 months | 21" | (53.5 cm) |
| 18 months | 22½" | (57 cm) |
| 24 months | 23¾" | (60.5 cm) |

***Size Note:*** Instructions are written for size 12 months, with sizes 18 and 24 months in braces { }. Instructions will be easier to read if you circle all the numbers pertaining to your size. If only one number is given, it applies to all sizes.

## Materials

Medium Weight Yarn (MEDIUM 4)
[6 ounces, 315 yards
(170 grams, 288 meters) per skein]:
MC (Yellow) - 1{1-2} skein(s)
[3 ounces, 157 yards
(85 grams, 144 meters) per skein]:
Color A (White) - 1 skein
Color B (Red) - 1 skein
Crochet hook, size G (4 mm) **or** size needed for gauge
Tapestry needle
Sewing needle and matching thread
¼" (7 mm) Buttons - 9

**Gauge:** In pattern, 5 V-Sts = 3" (7.5 cm) and 10 rows = 4" (10 cm)

**Gauge Swatch:** 3¼" x 4" (8.5 cm x 10 cm)
Ch 19.
Work same as Body for 10 rows.
Finish off.

## Stitch Guide

### V-St

(Dc, ch 1, dc) in stitch or space indicated.

## Body

Cardigan is worked in one piece to underarm.

With MC, ch 106{112-118}.

**Row 1:** Work V-St in fifth ch from hook **(4 skipped chs count as first dc plus 1 skipped ch)**, (skip next 2 chs, work V-St in next ch) across to last 2 chs, skip next ch, dc in last ch: 34{36-38} V-sts.

**Row 2** (Right side)**:** Ch 3 **(counts as first dc, now and throughout)**, turn; work V-St in each ch-1 sp across, dc in last dc.

Loop a short piece of yarn around any stitch to mark Row 2 as **right** side.

**Rows 3 thru 10{10-12}:** Repeat Row 2, 8{8-10} times; do **not** finish off.

## Left Front

**Row 1:** Ch 3, turn; work V-St in first 7{8-9} ch-1 sps, dc in next ch-1 sp, leave remaining sts unworked: 7{8-9} V-Sts.

**Row 2** (Decrease row)**:** Ch 3, turn; work V-St in each ch-1 sp across to last ch-1 sp, dc in last ch-1 sp and in next dc, leave last dc unworked: 6{7-8} V-Sts.

**Row 3:** Ch 3, turn; skip next 2 dc, work V-St in each ch-1 sp across, dc in last dc.

**Rows 4 thru 8{10-12}:** Repeat Rows 2 and 3, 2{3-4} times; then repeat Row 2 once **more**: 3 V-Sts.

Finish off leaving a long length for sewing.

## Back

**Row 1:** With **wrong** side facing, join MC with dc in first ch-1 sp after Left Front *(see Joining With Dc, page 30)*; work V-St in next 16 ch-1 sps, dc in next ch-1 sp: 16 V-Sts.

**Rows 2 thru 8{10-12}:** Ch 3, turn; work V-St in each ch-1 sp across, dc in last dc.

Finish off.

## Right Front

**Row 1:** With **wrong** side facing, join MC with dc in first ch-1 sp after Back; work V-St in each ch-1 sp across, dc in last dc: 7{8-9} V-Sts.

**Row 2** (Decrease row)**:** Ch 3, turn; dc in next ch-1 sp, work V-St in each ch-1 sp across, dc in last dc: 6{7-8} V-Sts.

**Row 3:** Ch 3, turn; work V-St in each ch-1 sp across, skip next 2 dc, dc in last dc.

**Rows 4-8:** Repeat Rows 2 and 3 twice, then repeat Row 2 once **more**: 3 V-Sts.

Finish off leaving a long length for sewing.

Whipstitch shoulder seams *(Fig. 5, page 31)*.

## Ruffle Edging

**Rnd 1:** With **right** side facing and working in free loops of beginning ch *(Fig. 2, page 30)*, join Color A with sc in first ch on Left Front *(see Joining With Sc, page 30)*; 2 sc in same st, sc in each ch across to last ch, 3 sc in last ch; sc evenly around increasing as necessary around curves to keep piece lying flat; join with slip st to first sc.

**Rnd 2:** Ch 4 **(counts as first tr, now and throughout)**, do **not** turn; tr in same sc, 2 tr in next sc and in each sc around; join with slip st to first tr, finish off.

## Sleeve (make 2)

Sleeve is worked across length.

With MC, ch 37{40-43}.

**Row 1:** Work V-St in fifth ch from hook, (skip next 2 chs, work V-St in next ch) across to last 2 chs, skip next ch, dc in last ch: 11{12-13} V-Sts.

**Row 2** (Right side)**:** Ch 3, turn; work V-St in each ch-1 sp across, dc in last dc.

Mark Row 2 as **right** side.

**Rows 3 thru 17{21-25}:** Repeat Row 2, 15{19-23} times.

Finish off leaving a long length for sewing.

With **right** sides together, fold Sleeve in half and whipstitch seam matching last row to beginning ch ***(Fig. 5, page 31)***; sew Sleeve to armhole placing seam at bottom of armhole and easing to fit.

### Cuff

**Rnd 1:** With **right** side facing and working in end of rows on Sleeve, join Color A with sc in first row; work 25{31-37} sc evenly spaced around; join with slip st to first sc: 26{32-38} sc.

**Rnd 2:** Ch 4, tr in same st, 2 tr in next sc and in each sc around; join with slip st to first tr; finish off: 52{64-76} tr.

## Appliqués

### Large Toadstool Cap

**Row 1** (Right side)**:** With Color B, ch 2, 3 sc in second ch from hook: 3 sc.

Mark Row 1 as **right** side.

**Row 2:** Ch 1, turn; 2 sc in each sc across: 6 sc.

**Row 3:** Ch 1, turn; sc in first sc, 2 sc in next sc, (sc in next sc, 2 sc in next sc) twice: 9 sc.

**Row 4:** Ch 1, turn; sc in first 2 sc, 2 sc in next sc, (sc in next 2 sc, 2 sc in next sc) twice: 12 sc.

**Row 5:** Ch 1, turn; sc in first 3 sc, 2 sc in next sc, (sc in next 3 sc, 2 sc in next sc) twice: 15 sc.

**Edging:** Ch 1, turn; sc in each sc across; ch 1, work 12 sc evenly spaced across end of rows; join with slip st to first sc finish off leaving a long length for sewing: 27 sc.

### Stem

**Row 1:** With **right** side facing and holding Cap upside down, skip first 4 sc and join Color A with sc in next sc; sc in next 3 sc, leave remaining sts unworked: 4 sc.

**Rows 2-4:** Ch 1, turn; sc in each sc across.

**Rows 5 and 6:** Ch 1, turn; 2 sc in first sc, sc in each sc across to last sc, 2 sc in last sc: 8 sc.

Finish off leaving a long length for sewing.

### Small Toadstool Cap

**Rows 1-3:** Work same as Large Toadstool: 9 sc.

**Edging:** Ch 1, turn; sc in each sc across; ch 1, 6 sc evenly spaced across end of rows; join with slip st to first sc, finish off leaving a long length for sewing: 15 sc.

### Stem

**Row 1:** With **right** side facing and holding Cap upside down, skip first 2 sc and join Color A with sc in next sc; sc in next sc, leave remaining sts unworked: 2 sc.

**Rows 2 and 3:** Ch 1, turn; sc in each sc across.

**Row 4:** Ch 1, turn; 2 sc in each sc; finish off leaving a long length for sewing: 4 sc.

Randomly sew 6 buttons on the Cap of the Large Toadstool, and 3 buttons on the Cap of the Small Toadstool, being sure to sew all buttons on firmly so baby cannot pull them off. Using photo as a guide for placement, pin Toadstools to front of cardigan, then sew in place.

# Ice Cream

INTERMEDIATE

| Sizes | Finished Chest Measurement | |
|---|---|---|
| 12 months | 21" | (53.5 cm) |
| 18 months | 22½" | (57 cm) |
| 24 months | 24" | (61 cm) |

***Size Note:*** Instructions are written for size 12 months, with sizes 18 and 24 months in braces { }. Instructions will be easier to read if you circle all the numbers pertaining to your size. If only one number is given, it applies to all sizes.

## Materials

Medium Weight Yarn (MEDIUM 4)

[6 ounces, 315 yards (170 grams, 288 meters) per skein]:
MC (Pink) - 1{1-2} skein(s)

[3 ounces, 157 yards (85 grams, 144 meters) per skein]:
Color A (Yellow) - small amount

[5 ounces, 249 yards (142 grams, 227 meters) per skein]:
Color B (Brown) - small amount

Crochet hook, size E (3.5 mm) for size 12 months, F (3.75 mm) for size 18 months, **or** G (4 mm) for size 24 months **or** size needed for gauge

Tapestry needle

Sewing needle and matching thread

3/8" (10 mm) wide Grosgrain Ribbon - 20" (51 cm)

**Gauge:** In pattern, 2 ripples = 3½{3¾-4}" (9{9.5-10} cm) and 10{9-9} rows = 4" (10 cm)

**Gauge Swatch:** 4{4¼-4½}" x 4" (10{11-11.5} cm x 10 cm)

Ch 20.

Work same as Back for 10{9-9} rows.

Finish off.

***Note:*** Cardigan pieces are worked from shoulders to lower edge. Different sizes are made by changing size of hook.

## Stitch Guide

### Picot

Ch 3, slip st in third ch from hook.

## BACK

With MC, ch 52.

**Row 1** (Right side and neck edge)**:** Dc in fourth ch from hook **(3 skipped chs count as first dc, now and throughout)** and in next 3 chs, skip next ch, dc in next 3 chs, ★ 3 dc in next ch, dc in next 3 chs, skip next ch, dc in next 3 chs; repeat from ★ across to last ch, 2 dc in last ch: 55 dc.

Loop a short piece of yarn around any dc to mark Row 1 as **right** side.

**Rows 2 thru 17{19-19}:** Ch 3 **(counts as first dc, now and when not used in a Picot)**, turn; dc in first 4 dc, skip next 2 dc, dc in next 3 dc, ★ 3 dc in next dc, dc in next 3 dc, skip next 2 dc, dc in next 3 dc; repeat from ★ across to last dc, 2 dc in last dc.

**Row 18{20-20}:** Ch 3, turn; slip st in third ch from hook (first Picot made), skip first dc, sc in next 3 dc, ★ skip next 2 dc, sc in next 4 dc, work Picot, sc in next 3 dc; repeat from ★ across to last 6 dc, skip next 2 dc, sc in next 3 dc, work Picot, slip st in last dc; finish off.

## RIGHT FRONT

With MC, ch 17.

**Row 1** (Right side)**:** Dc in fourth ch from hook and in next 3 chs, skip next ch, dc in next 3 chs, 3 dc in next ch, dc in next 3 chs, skip next ch, dc in last ch: 15 dc.

Mark Row 1 as **right** side.

**Row 2:** Ch 3, turn; skip next dc, dc in next 3 dc, 3 dc in next dc, dc in next 3 dc, skip next 2 dc, dc in next 3 dc, 2 dc in last dc.

**Row 3:** Ch 3, turn; dc in same dc and in next 3 dc, skip next 2 dc, dc in next 3 dc, 3 dc in next dc, dc in next 3 dc, skip next dc, dc in last dc.

**Row 4** (Neck shaping)**:** Ch 11, turn; dc in fifth ch from hook **(4 skipped chs count as first dc and skipped ch)**, dc in next 2 chs, 3 dc in next ch, dc in last 3 chs, skip next 2 dc, dc in next 3 dc, 3 dc in next dc, dc in next 3 dc, skip next 2 dc, dc in next 3 dc, 2 dc in last dc: 24 dc.

**Row 5:** Ch 3, turn; dc in first 4 dc ★ skip next 2 dc, dc in next 3 dc, 3 dc in next dc, dc in next 3 dc; repeat from ★ once **more**, skip next dc, dc in last dc.

**Row 6:** Ch 3, turn; skip next dc, dc in next 3 dc, ★ 3 dc in next dc, dc in next 3 dc, skip next 2 dc, dc in next 3 dc; repeat from ★ once **more**, 2 dc in last dc.

**Rows 7-17{19-19}:** Repeat Rows 5 and 6, 5{6-6} times; then repeat Row 5 once **more**.

**Row 18{20-20}:** Ch 3, turn; slip st in third ch from hook, sc in first dc, skip next sc, ★ sc in next 4 dc, Picot, sc in next 3 sc, skip next 2 sc; repeat from ★ once **more**, sc in next 4 dc, skip next dc, sc in next dc, Picot, slip st in last dc; finish off.

## Left Front

Work same as Right Front, marking Row 2 as **right** side.

## Sleeve (Make 2)

With MC, ch 36.

**Row 1** (Right side and Armhole edge)**:** Dc in fourth ch from hook and in next 3 chs, skip next ch, dc in next 3 chs, ★ 3 dc in next ch, dc in next 3 chs, skip next ch, dc in next 3 chs; repeat from ★ across to last ch, 2 dc in last ch: 37 dc.

Mark Row 1 as **right** side.

**Rows 2 thru 14{15-16}:** Ch 3, turn; dc in first 4 dc, skip next 2 dc, dc in next 3 dc, ★ 3 dc in next dc, dc in next 3 dc, skip next 2 dc, dc in next 3 dc; repeat from ★ across to last dc, 2 dc in last dc.

**Row 15{16-17}:** Ch 3, turn; slip st in third ch from hook, sc in first 4 dc, ★ skip next 2 dc, sc in next 4 dc, work Picot, sc in next 3 dc; repeat from ★ across to last 6 dc, skip next 2 dc, sc in next 3 dc, work Picot, sc in last dc; finish off leaving a long length for sewing.

## Finishing

Whipstitch shoulder seams *(Fig. 5, page 31)*.

Whipstitch Sleeves to cardigan, matching center of Row 1 on Sleeve to shoulder seam and beginning 3½{3¾-4}" (9{9.5-10} cm) down from shoulder seam.

Whipstitch Sleeve and side in one continuous seam.

## Appliqués

### Polka Dot

Make 11 with Color A and 11 with Color B.

**Rnd 1** (Right side)**:** Ch 2, 6 sc in second ch from hook; join with slip st to first sc.

**Rnd 2:** Ch 1, do **not** turn; 2 sc in Back Loop Only *(Fig. 1, page 30)* of each sc around; join with slip st to first sc; finish off leaving a long length for sewing: 12 sc.

### Picot Polka Dot

Make 5 with Color A and 5 with Color B.

**Rnd 1** (Right side)**:** Ch 2, 6 sc in second ch from hook; join with slip st to first sc.

**Rnd 2:** Ch 1, do **not** turn; 2 sc in Back Loop Only of each sc around; join with slip st to first sc: 12 sc.

**Rnd 3:** Work Picot, skip next sc, (slip st in Back Loop Only of next sc, work Picot, skip next sc) around, join with slip st to joining slip st; finish off leaving a long length for sewing.

Using photo as a guide for placement, pin appliqués to cardigan, doing one section at a time, and then sew in place.

Weave ribbon through the space between the first 2 dc on Row 5 of each Front and tie in a bow; trim ends if desired.

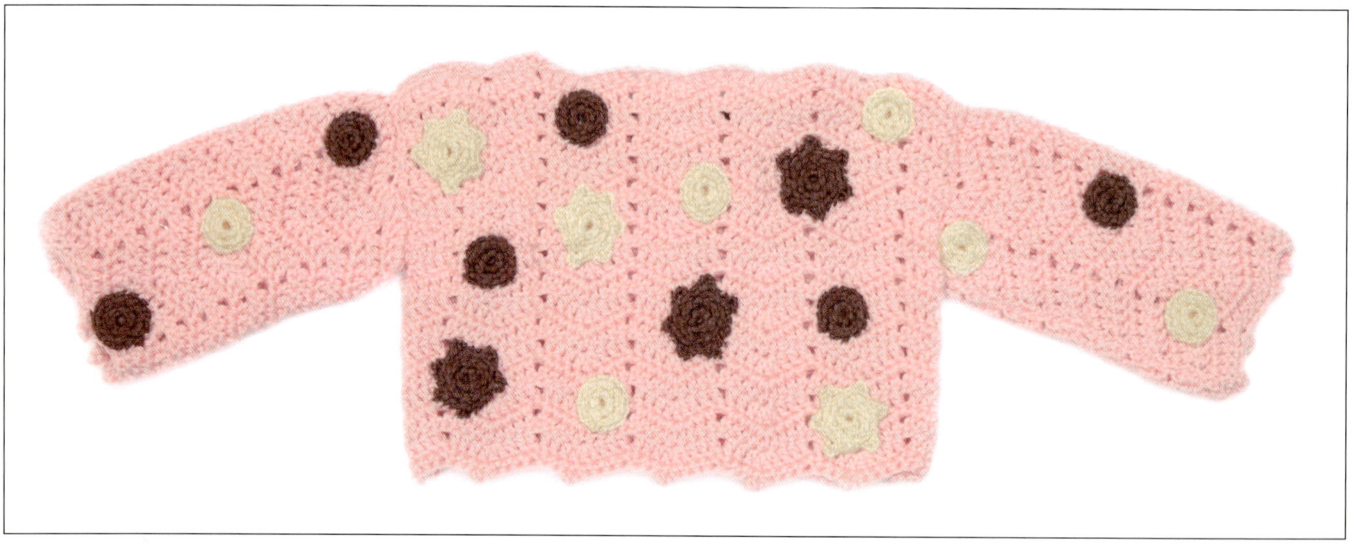

# GENERAL INSTRUCTIONS

| | |
|---|---|
| BEGINNER | Projects for first-time knitters using basic knit and purl stitches. Minimal shaping. |
| EASY | Projects using basic stitches, repetitive stitch patterns, simple color changes, and simple shaping and finishing. |
| INTERMEDIATE | Projects with a variety of stitches, such as basic cables and lace, simple intarsia, double-pointed needles and knitting in the round needle techniques, mid-level shaping and finishing. |
| EXPERIENCED | Projects using advanced techniques and stitches, such as short rows, fair isle, more intricate intarsia, cables, lace patterns, and numerous color changes. |

| Yarn Weight Symbol & Names | LACE 0 | SUPER FINE 1 | FINE 2 | LIGHT 3 | MEDIUM 4 | BULKY 5 | SUPER BULKY 6 |
|---|---|---|---|---|---|---|---|
| Type of Yarns in Category | Fingering, 10-count crochet thread | Sock, Fingering Baby | Sport, Baby | DK, Light Worsted | Worsted, Afghan, Aran | Chunky, Craft, Rug | Bulky, Roving |
| Crochet Gauge* Ranges in Single Crochet to 4" (10 cm) | 32-42 double crochets** | 21-32 sts | 16-20 sts | 12-17 sts | 11-14 sts | 8-11 sts | 5-9 sts |
| Advised Hook Size Range | Steel*** 6,7,8 Regular hook B-1 | B-1 to E-4 | E-4 to 7 | 7 to I-9 | I-9 to K-10.5 | K-10.5 to M-13 | M-13 and larger |

*GUIDELINES ONLY: The chart above reflects the most commonly used gauges and hook sizes for specific yarn categories.

** Lace weight yarns are usually crocheted on larger-size hooks to create lacy openwork patterns. Accordingly, a gauge range is difficult to determine. Always follow the gauge stated in your pattern.

*** Steel crochet hooks are sized differently from regular hooks–the higher the number the smaller the hook, which is the reverse of regular hook sizing.

| CROCHET HOOKS | | | | | | | | | | | | | |
|---|---|---|---|---|---|---|---|---|---|---|---|---|---|
| **Metrics mm** | 2.25 | 2.75 | 3.25 | 3.5 | 3.75 | 4 | 5 | 5.5 | 6 | 6.5 | 9 | 10 | 15 |
| **U.S.** | B-1 | C-2 | D-3 | E-4 | F-5 | G-6 | H-8 | I-9 | J-10 | K-10½ | N | P | Q |

| CROCHET TERMINOLOGY | | |
|---|---|---|
| UNITED STATES | = | INTERNATIONAL |
| slip stitch (slip st) | = | single crochet (sc) |
| single crochet (sc) | = | double crochet (dc) |
| half double crochet (hdc) | = | half treble crochet (htr) |
| double crochet (dc) | = | treble crochet(tr) |
| treble crochet (tr) | = | double treble crochet (dtr) |
| double treble crochet (dtr) | = | triple treble crochet (ttr) |
| triple treble crochet (tr tr) | = | quadruple treble crochet (qtr) |
| skip | = | miss |

## Abbreviations

| | |
|---|---|
| **CC** | Contrasting Color |
| **ch(s)** | chain(s) |
| **cm** | centimeters |
| **dc** | double crochet(s) |
| **hdc** | half double crochet(s) |
| **MC** | Main Color |
| **mm** | millimeters |
| **Rnd(s)** | Round(s) |
| **sc** | single crochet(s) |
| **sp(s)** | space(s) |
| **st(s)** | stitch(es) |
| **tr** | treble crochet(s) |
| **YO** | yarn over |

★ - work instructions following ★ as many **more** times as indicated in addition to the first time.

**( ) or [ ]** - work enclosed instructions **as many** times as specified by the number immediately following **or** work all enclosed instructions in the stitch or space indicated **or** contains explanatory remarks.

**colon (:)** - the number(s) given after a colon at the end of a row or round denote(s) the number of stitches you should have on that row or round.

## Gauge

Exact gauge is **essential** for proper fit. Before beginning your project, make the sample swatch given in the individual instructions in the yarn or thread and hook specified. After completing the swatch, measure it, counting your stitches and rows carefully. If your swatch is larger or smaller than specified, **make another, changing hook size to get the correct gauge.** Keep trying until you find the size hook that will give you the specified gauge. Once proper gauge is obtained, measure width of garment approximately every 3" (7.5 cm) to be sure gauge remains consistent.

## Zeros

To consolidate the length of an involved pattern, Zeros are sometimes used so that all sizes can be combined. For example, increase every sixth row 5{1-0} time(s) means the first size would increase 5 times, the second size would increase once, and the largest size would do nothing.

## Joining With SC

When instructed to join with sc, begin with a slip knot on hook. Insert hook in stitch or space indicated, YO and pull up a loop, YO and draw through both loops on hook.

## Joining With DC

When instructed to join with dc, begin with a slip knot on hook. YO, holding loop on hook, insert hook in stitch or space indicated, YO and pull up a loop (3 loops on hook), (YO and draw through 2 loops on hook) twice.

## Back or Front Loop Only

Work only in loop(s) indicated by arrow ***(Fig. 1)***.

**Fig. 1**

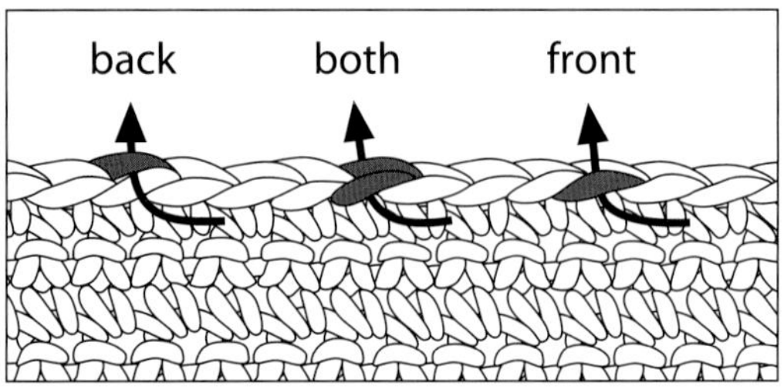


## Free Loops of a Chain

When instructed to work in free loops of a chain, work in loop indicated by arrow ***(Fig. 2)***.

**Fig. 2**

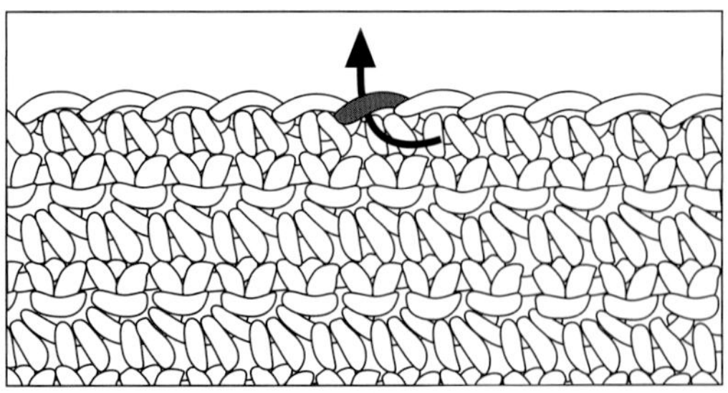

## Vorking Around Previous Row

Vork in stitch or space indicated, inserting hook in irection of arrow ***(Fig. 3)***.

**Fig. 3**

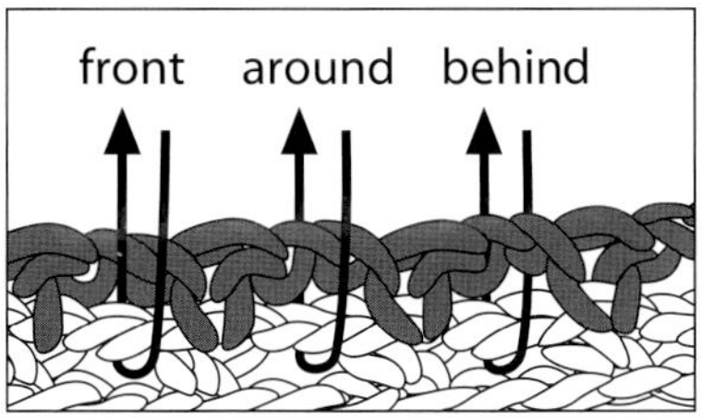


## :hanging Colors

nsert hook in stitch indicated, YO and pull up a loop, rop yarn, with new yarn ***(Fig. 4)***, YO and draw through oth loops on hook.

Vork over color not being used, holding it with normal ension.

**Fig. 4**

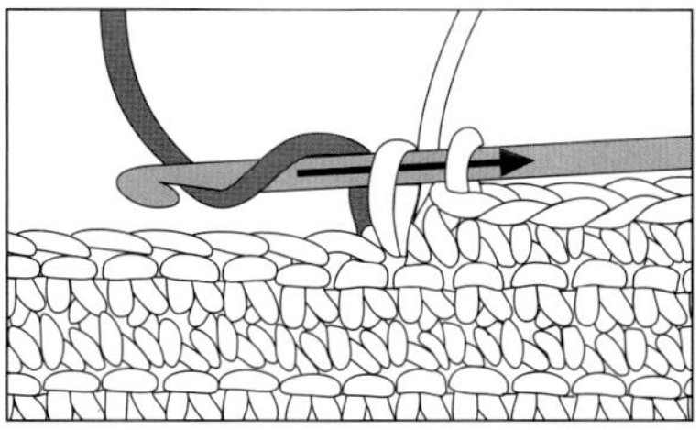

## Vhipstitch

Vith wrong sides together, sew through both pieces once secure the beginning of the seam, leaving an ample arn end to weave in later. Insert the needle from right to ft through one strand on each piece ***(Fig. 5)***. Bring the eedle around and insert it from right to left through e next strand on both pieces.

epeat along the edge, being careful to match stitches nd rows.

**Fig. 5**

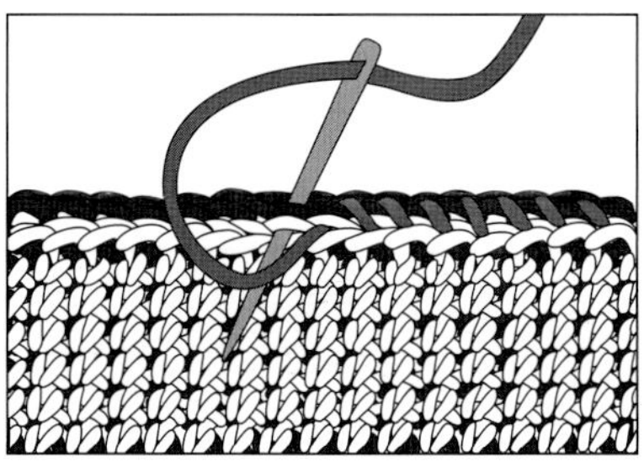

## French Knot

Bring needle up at 1. Wrap thread or embroidery floss around needle the desired number of times and insert needle at 2, holding end of thread or floss with non-stitching fingers ***(Fig. 6)***. Tighten knot; then pull needle through, holding thread or floss until it must be released.

**Fig. 6**

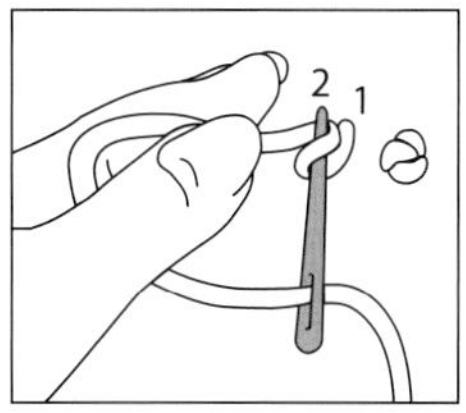


## Backstitch

The Backstitch is worked from right to left. Come up at 1, go down at 2 and come up at 3 ***(Fig. 7)***. The second stitch is made by going down at 1 and coming up at 4.

**Fig. 7**

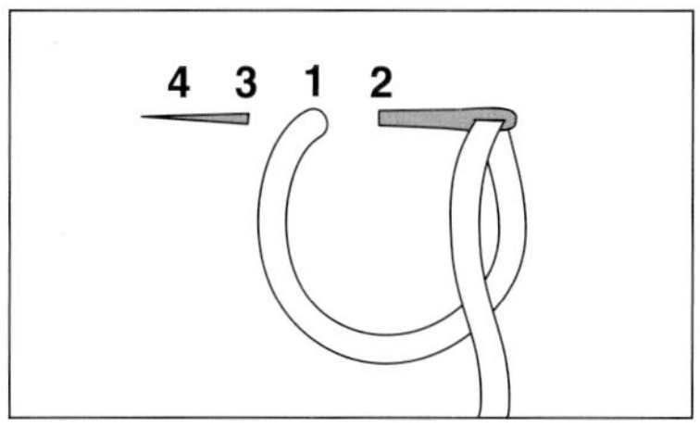

# Yarn Information

The items in this leaflet were made using a variety of yarns or threads. Any brand of the specific weight of yarn or thread may be used. It is best to refer to the yardage/meters when determining how many balls or skeins to purchase. Remember, to achieve the same look, it is the weight of yarn that is important, not the brand of yarn.

For your convenience, listed below are the specific yarns used to create our photography models.

## Bead Toy

***Caron® Simply Soft®***

MC (White) - #9701 White

Color A (Pink) - #2614 Pink

Color B (Blue) - #2615 Soft Blue

## Monkeying Around

***J&P Coats® Royale® Fashion Crochet size 3***

MC - #0065 Warm Teal

***J&P Coats® Royale® Classic Crochet size 10***

Tan - #310 Copper Mist

Cream - #420 Cream

Red - #494 Victory Red

## Breakfast on the Farm

***Red Heart® Lustersheen®***

MC (Red) - #0915 Cherry Red

A (White) - #0001 White

B (Yellow) - #0227 Buttercup

C (Black) - #0002 Black

## Fairy Tale Forest

***Caron® Simply Soft®***

MC (Yellow) - #9702 Off White

Color A (White) - #2601 White

Color B (Red) - #2721 Autumn Red

## Ice Cream

***Caron® Simply Soft®***

MC (Pink) - #9721 Pink

Color A (Yellow) - #9702 Off White

***Caron® Simply Soft®Eco***

Color B (Brown) - #0006 Chocolate

We have made every effort to ensure that these instructions are accurate and complete. We cannot, however, be responsible for human error, typographical mistakes, or variations in individual work.


## Production Team

**Technical Writer/Editor** - Joan Beebe, Jean Guirguis, Peggy Greig; **Editorial Writer** - Susan McManus Johnson; **Senior Graphic Artist** - Lora Puls; **Graphic Artist** - Jane Fay; **Photography Manager** - Katherine Laughlin; **Photo Stylist** - Sondra Daniel; and **Photographer** - Ken West.


## Digital Downloads

To obtain digital copies of Leisure Arts' best-selling designs, visit **http://www.leisureartslibrary.com**